Little Science

Weather Chart

By Amanda Gebhardt

Look up at the sky.
What can you see?

Can you see the Sun?
Will it rain?

4

Stand outside. What
can you feel?

Is it hot? Can you
feel wind blow?

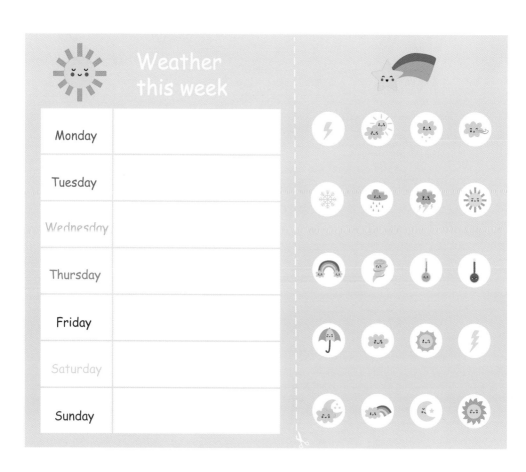

Weather this week

Monday	
Tuesday	
Wednesday	
Thursday	
Friday	
Saturday	
Sunday	

Keep track with this chart.
Get help if you need it.

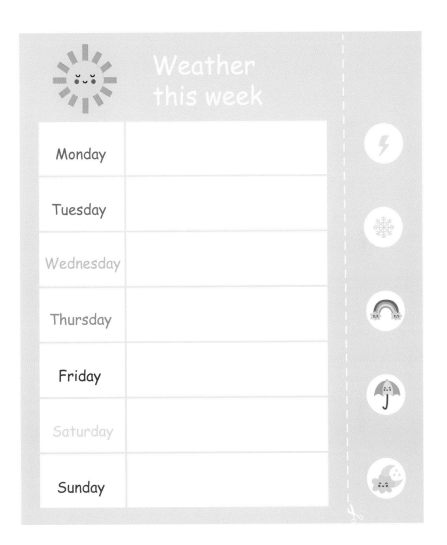

Weather this week

Monday	
Tuesday	
Wednesday	
Thursday	
Friday	
Saturday	
Sunday	

Make a box for each day this week.

Look up. What can you see?
What can you feel?

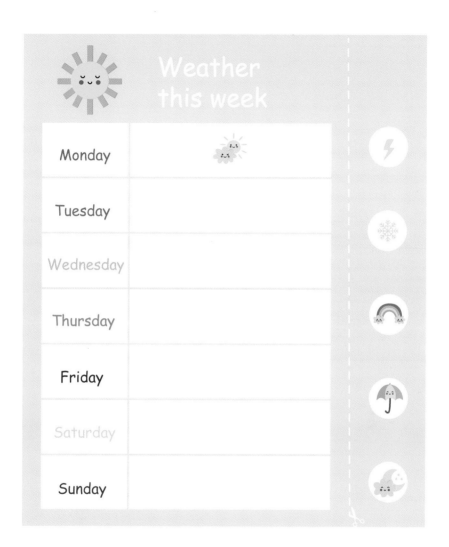

Weather this week

Monday	
Tuesday	
Wednesday	
Thursday	
Friday	
Saturday	
Sunday	

**Write it in this box.
Make it look neat.**

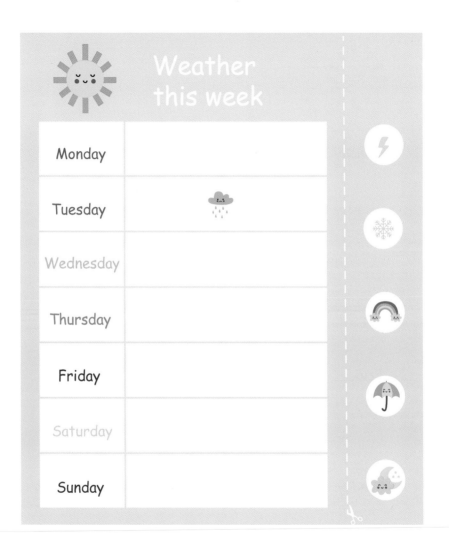

Weather this week

Monday	
Tuesday	
Wednesday	
Thursday	
Friday	
Saturday	
Sunday	

10 **Wait for the next day. Write what you can see and feel.**

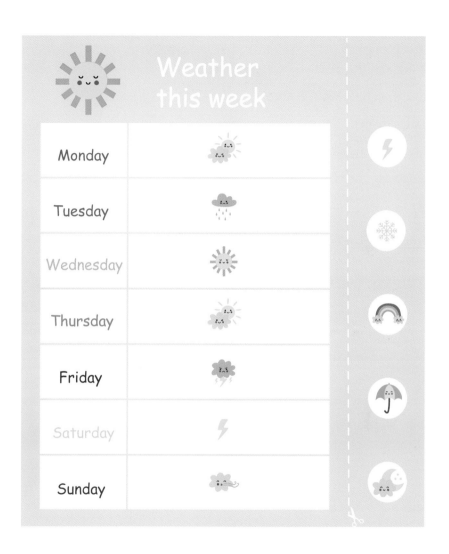

Weather this week

Monday	
Tuesday	
Wednesday	
Thursday	
Friday	
Saturday	
Sunday	

**Write this each day this week.
Then look at each box.**

Tell what the weather was
like this week.

Was it the same? Did it change?

Word List

science words

change	Sun
chart	track
rain	weather
sky	wind

sight words

a	the
change	was
chart	Was
for	weather
outside	What
sky	what

Vowel Teams

/ā/ai, ay	/ē/ea, ee	/ō/ow
day	each	blow
rain	feel	
Wait	Keep	/o͞o/ou
	neat	you
	need	
	see	/o͝o/oo
	week	Look
		look

Try It!
Make a weather chart. Track the weather for a week.
Tell if the weather changed or stayed the same.

107 Words

Look up at the sky. What can you see?

Can you see the Sun? Will it rain?

Stand outside. What can you feel?

Is it hot? Can you feel wind blow?

Keep track with this chart. Get help if you need it.

Make a box for each day this week.

Look up. What can you see? What can you feel?

Write it in this box. Make it look neat.

Wait for the next day. Write what you can see and feel.

Write this each day this week. Then look at each box.

Tell what the weather was like this week.

Was it the same? Did it change?

CHERRY BLOSSOM PRESS

Published in the United States of America by Cherry Lake Publishing Group
Ann Arbor, Michigan
www.cherrylakepublishing.com

Photo Credits: © Natchar Lai/Shutterstock, cover, title page; © Krotnakro/Shutterstock, 2; © Evgeniy_16/Shutterstock, 3; © Monkey Business Images/Dreamstime.com, 4; © Monika Gniot/ Shutterstock, 5; © Milya Shaykh/Shutterstock, 6–11, back cover; © Anna Kraynova/Shutterstock, 8; © Monkey Business Images/Dreamstime.com, 12; © Monkey Business Images/Dreamstime.com, 13

Cherry Blossom Press is an imprint of Cherry Lake Publishing Group.

Library of Congress Cataloging-in-Publication Data

Names: Gebhardt, Amanda, author.
Title: Weather chart / written by Amanda Gebhardt.
Description: Ann Arbor, Michigan : Cherry Blossom Press, [2024] | Series:
    Little science stories | Audience: Grades K-1 | Summary: "Learn how to
    build a weather chart in this decodable science book for beginning
    readers. A combination of domain-specific sight words and sequenced
    phonics skills builds confidence in content area reading. Bold, colorful
    photographs align directly with the text to help readers strengthen
    comprehension"– Provided by publisher.
Identifiers: LCCN 2023035040 | ISBN 9781668937716 (paperback) | ISBN
    9781668940099 (ebook) | ISBN 9781668941447 (pdf)
Subjects: LCSH: Weather–Juvenile literature. | Weather–Physiological
    effect–Juvenile literature.
Classification: LCC QC981.3 .G44 2024 | DDC 551.6022/3–dc23/eng/20231005
LC record available at https://lccn.loc.gov/2023035040

Printed in the United States of America

Amanda Gebhardt is a curriculum writer and editor and a life-long learner. She lives in Ann Arbor, Michigan, with her husband, two kids, and one playful pup named Cookie.